Puppy Parenting Basics

CASSIE LEIGH

CONTENTS

Introduction   1

Breed Matters   3

The Cost Of Owning A Dog   7

Buy A Dog Or Rescue A Dog   9

Naming Your Pup   15

What You're Going To Need For You   17

What You're Going To Need For The Pup   21

Preparing Your House   33

Establish A Routine   35

Expose Your Dog To Different Experiences   37

The Go Bag   39

Additional Items For The Park   43

Additional Items For The Dog Park   47

Dog Park Etiquette   49

Exercising Your Dog   51

Toys—General   53

Toys—The Noise Issue   55

Training Your Pup   57

Pulling Crap Out Of Your Pup's Mouth   61

Puke And Poop   63

A Good Veterinarian Is Worth Their Weight In Gold   65

Spay Or Neuter Your Dog   67

Riding In The Car   69

Feeding Your Dog Human Food   73

What To Do For A Sick Stomach   75

Make Friends   77

Dealing With Children   79

Conclusion   81

INTRODUCTION

Last year I wrote a book called *Puppy Parenting in an Apartment*. Why? Because it's what I knew.

The first year I had my Newfie puppy, Miss Priss, we lived in two different apartments. And I had to learn a number of tricks to manage that experience that I'd never really had to consider when I was growing up and we had dogs in our house.

I didn't figure I could speak to the experience of raising a puppy in a house because that's not what I'd done. But...I've been getting feedback from readers of the original puppy parenting book that a lot of the topics I cover in there are relevant to anyone trying to raise a puppy anywhere. (The tears, the struggle, the lack of sleep...Haha. Just kidding. Although, that too.)

So I've gone through that original puppy parenting book and extracted the bits I think apply to everyone raising a new puppy. And, now that pup and I live in a house with a yard and some family members have recently gone through the new puppy experience while living in a house, I touch on some house-related puppy parenting issues, too.

I love my pup. I upended my world for her. But those early days? Man, they were HARD. I had this adorable little ball of fur that was just the cutest damned thing. Except for when she was biting me with those little razor-sharp puppy teeth. Or crying her poor little heart out at three in the morning. Or lying down and refusing to move halfway through her walk. Or puking. Or...yeah.

You've been there, too, haven't you? And if you haven't yet, well, you will be. (My girl was an angel compared to many pups, but that doesn't mean it was easy to raise her.)

So, if you're thinking of getting a pup or just bought one, this book will help. It's full of tips and tricks to make things a little bit easier.

We'll start with a few things to consider before you even bring home that adorable little ball of fur.

BREED MATTERS

One of the most important factors in raising your puppy will occur before you even bring that pup home. And that's what breed of dog you choose.

You should think long and hard about this. Read as much as you can about the breed. Is it social? Does it do well with children? What about with other dogs? How intelligent is it? How much activity does it need? Is it a highly social type of dog or a loner?

And what about size? How big is that dog going to get?

And then ask yourself—does that work for me and my lifestyle?

I was very fortunate with the pup because I didn't choose her. My mom bought the pup for herself and then my mom's existing dog (a breed known for being territorial) attacked the pup and my mom had to find her a new home. Fortunately for me, pup was exactly the kind of dog I wanted.

She's a mellow, intelligent dog. She likes to go for a walk and run around in the yard, but she also sleeps for hours every single day so I have plenty of time to work. She's a big dog— about a hundred pounds—which is what I prefer. (I always worry I'd step on one of those tiny little dogs.)

So things worked out for me.

But I have friends who have dogs that would never, ever work for me. And pup would not be ideal for a few of the folks I know.

For example, one of the ladies at the dog park we used to go to had some sort of racing breed of dog. She'd run the dog to the dog park, let it play for an hour, run it home, and it would still want attention. An active dog like that living with a lazy person like me would make both of us miserable.

And pup is a hot mess a lot of the time. She'll wallow in a mud puddle if it has the littlest bit of water in it or race through the middle of a wet meadow if something looks interesting. Works for me. I just wipe her down and try to remember to vacuum every once in a while. But one of my friends has an all-white house—from the carpet to the towels to the walls. Pup would be her version of hell on earth.

Also think about what kind of maintenance your dog will require. I have to brush the pup often and, during early spring, I end up spending a good half hour every day pulling grass seed out of her toes after we go to the dog park. A smooth-coated breed that doesn't have webbed toes probably wouldn't have that issue. (But it might shed like crazy if my experience petting other dogs at the dog park is any indication.)

So, really think about it before you choose that dog. You want a dog that you'll enjoy and a dog that will enjoy your lifestyle.

Another thing to consider is how easy that dog is going to be to train and whether you can handle it. Newfies love to please and respond well to praise and treats. That means house-training her was very, very easy. Other dogs? Not so much.

She's also very intelligent, which is great, because I can't stand dogs that aren't, but it's also a challenge. I can't trick pup into doing anything more than once. She recently became scared of PetSmart after a bad grooming experience. I was able to feed her McDonald's hash browns to lure her through the front door once. The next trip? Uh-uh. Wasn't having it. She knew exactly what I was trying to do, so I had to come up with another plan. And next time we go? I'll need yet another plan.

(It makes giving her any sort of medicine a bit of a challenge, let me tell you. Thankfully, she really, really likes peanut butter and was smart enough to learn that if she licked all the peanut butter off the pill then my only choice was to give her a pill by triggering her gag reflex.)

Also, think about diseases and illnesses that the breed is prone to. A lot of a dog's health is up to you and how you treat the dog, but some health issues will be out of your control. For each breed of dog there are health risks that come with the breed. For example, golden retrievers are very prone to developing cancer. And pup has recently developed some very mild knee dysplasia, something her breed is prone to. (Most of the Newfs we've met have some degree of hip dysplasia, another ailment her breed is prone to.)

So, know going in what you're up against.

Another sad fact about the larger breeds is that they don't live as long as the smaller breeds. Can you handle having that dog for only seven or eight years?

On the flip side of that, if you think you'll retire in ten years, are you prepared to have a dog that lives sixteen years? Or would you be better off with a breed that lives a shorter period of time and will be gone by the time you retire?

And be aware that there may be restrictions on what breed of dog you're allowed where you live. Here in Colorado, for example, almost every city in the metro area of Denver bans pit bulls. Many apartment buildings ban breeds prone to aggression (like pit bulls) as well as dogs that are known to be loud. The list can be somewhat surprising, so be sure to check before you bring your dog home.

Many apartment buildings also limit how big your dog can be or how many dogs you can have. (The most common limits I've seen are either twenty-five pounds or seventy-five pounds.)

Before you commit to that dog, make sure you actually can. And, please, be prepared to commit to the dog for its entire life. Dogs are loyal, loving creatures and they deserve owners that will be as loyal and loving to them.

I once knew a woman who said that she never kept a dog once it got old because she didn't want to see the dog die. I thought that was the worst thing I'd ever heard. Here this dog had loved her and her family and when it got old she just gave it away, meaning it died away from everyone it had known and loved its whole life.

Dogs do have emotions even if they can't speak and tell you what they're feeling, so spare a thought for that dog before you accept responsibility for it. (And after.)

THE COST OF OWNING A DOG

I'm not going to tell you how much it costs to own a dog because that will depend very much on what kind of dog you buy, where you live, how you treat that dog, and what health issues the dog does or does not have.

I was fortunate because I got the pup for free. My brother and his wife were given one of their dogs and bought the other for $50 at a pet event. On the other hand, I dated a guy once who was planning on importing some dog that was only bred overseas. He was going to pay something like seven thousand dollars for the dog.

There's also a tremendous range of costs for feeding a dog. My pup is close to a hundred pounds and we go through a bag of Eukanuba about once a month, so her basic food costs me maybe $50 a month. But there was a point there where I had her on some sort of fancy wet dog food for an irritable stomach and that was much, much more expensive. You also have to factor in the cost of things like treats. I have five varieties of treats that I give the pup on a regular basis. (I know. She's spoiled as hell.)

And then there's medical costs. In the first year I owned the pup I think I spent over a thousand dollars on vet bills. ($400 of that was one stupid vet visit that I still regret to this day.)

Now that we've settled into things a little more, it's less, but we've still been to the vet a few times this year. And because I do board her and take her to the dog park and day care, she has to have more shots than a dog that just stays home all the time.

At a minimum, you can expect to need rabies shots for your dog. And most will need Bordetella at some point. There's also flea/tick medicine and heart worm medicine.

And expect to spay/neuter your dog. And possibly pay for food supplements or medicines as the dog ages.

Finally, how much will you spend on bedding, clothing, and toys? That's very much up to you and how you choose to treat your dog.

Just don't think that the last money you're really going to spend is when you buy your dog.

BUY A DOG OR RESCUE A DOG

I'm going to confess to something that a certain population of dog owners will hate: Almost all of our family dogs when I was growing up came from pet stores. Generally, we'd be at the mall, see a cute puppy in the window, and, with lots of tears and begging, end up with a dog.

I know there are reasons people object to buying dogs at the pet store. (Some of them source their dogs from puppy mills.) And I agree that puppy mills and the conditions they subject puppies to are horrible. But not all puppies at pet stores come from puppy mills, and there are some advantages to buying a dog through a pet store as opposed to rescuing a dog, which is, of course, the more noble, socially accepted way of doing things.

My mom bought the pup at a pet store. And, because of that, all the medical issues that occurred with her in the first month were covered by the pet store. She was also as much of a blank slate as a puppy can be in terms of behaviors and training, which meant there was no need to overcome older ingrained bad habits.

There are potential issues with house training a puppy that comes from a pet store. Some of the dogs, because they do sleep in smaller areas with other dogs so can't really designate an area for their waste, lose a dog's natural aversion to pooping and peeing in its own area. This can make crate training harder, because the dog will do its business in its crate even if that means the dog has to lay in it. But with pup I never saw that happen.

Then again, I was home with her and we didn't crate train, so she was never really forced into a small space like that.

You can also buy from a breeder. My brother did that with his St. Bernards and it worked out very well. They were able to cut out that middle step with the pet store and see exactly where the pups had been born and raised. It also gave them much more information about the pups' parents and any health issues they might've had.

I know another couple who bought their Newfies through a breeder. One worked out great, but two others had to be returned—one for a serious heart issue the breed is prone to and another for a severe overbite.

In general, going to a breeder is probably the best, most problem-free route to take. I think it can also be fairly expensive, though.

And if you do go this route and the dog is considered show-quality and the breeder wants you to agree to let them show the dog, I wouldn't recommend that. I knew a guy who did this and he said that the training the dog underwent to be show-trained made the dog a less than ideal pet. Show dogs are trained to sit and act in a certain way and it seems the dog was never able to turn off that training when it was home with him.

Your third option is a rescue dog. This has the advantage of doing something really good for a dog who didn't get a great start.

Because the pup and I are out and about a lot, we've met a number of rescued dogs. (I swear, every dog we met in the D.C. area was a rescue. It was crazy. Maybe the only people who take their dogs to dog parks in D.C. are people who rescue dogs. Although rescuing a dog is also a very D.C. thing to do, too.)

When I was growing up, we had a rescue dog. She was fantastic, but not without her issues. (In her case, a fear of men and seizures for the first few years we owned her.)

So, rescues can be great and you are doing something wonderful by taking on a dog someone else abandoned, but rescues can present some difficult challenges. What challenges exactly?

1. Attachment Issues

This can come in a few flavors.

One dog I knew wouldn't let the dog walker walk him. The guy would show up and the dog would hide. Which meant the owner had a problem, because she had to leave the dog alone for long hours, but the dog wouldn't let anyone but her take him outside. That meant it was more likely that the dog would mess in her apartment and it added pressure to his owner because she knew that the only way that dog was going to get outside was if she went home and took him out herself.

Another dog I knew hated PetSmart. He'd been taken there for adoption events so associated the place with that negative experience and would refuse to go through the doors.

That would've been a problem for me for a couple of reasons. First, when pup and I lived in the apartment, there were times she just needed to get outside. But in the summer in DC when it was 95 degrees out, I couldn't exactly take her for a walk around the neighborhood. What I could do was run her up to PetSmart and walk her around inside for a bit. Also, that's who I used for doggie daycare.

I knew another dog who never let his owner out of his sight. He was so scared of being abandoned, his owner literally couldn't be more than about five feet from him before he'd get upset.

2. Socialization Issues

Now, PetSmart isn't the only option for doggie daycare, but that brings up another complication parents of rescues face. Often the dogs have issues playing with other dogs. Sometimes it's as simple as just not knowing how to. Some rescues were never raised around other dogs, so just don't know what to do when another dog tries to play with them. Good news is those dogs *can* learn over time what to do.

But some rescue dogs are aggressive towards other dogs, which means you won't be able to take them to day care anywhere. (Now, that's fine. When I was growing up we never felt the need to take our dogs to day care. They just hung around the house while we were away. Me, however....Well...If it's going to be more than four or five hours, I like to take the pup somewhere where she can interact with people or dogs rather than stay at home all alone even though she'd probably just sleep.)

3. Aggression Issues

I mentioned the obvious one above. Some rescues are aggressive towards other dogs because they were never properly socialized. (I even heard of a rescue who killed one of the other dogs in the family that adopted it.)

That's bad enough, but some dogs have aggression issues with people, too.

That rescue we had when I was a kid actually bit my grandfather. I was a baby at the time and he threw me in the air, as you do with babies (not HIGH, just a little toss to make me squeal). Well, the dog bit him. Because where she came from, men were mean and abusive and a man doing something like that to a baby wasn't playing with the baby but was instead harming the baby.

You need to be very careful about bringing a rescue dog into your family. Many are wonderful, wonderful dogs, but don't be naïve about it.

4. Fear Issues

The flip-side to the aggression issue is that some rescues will be scared of people in your household. Generally, and this is generally, the dog will be scared of men. Why? Well...Unfortunately, men tend to be the ones who are more violent towards dogs.

See, the thing is, dogs have amazingly good memories. They don't forget what they experience. (We're three months out from pup's grooming experience and she still won't go through the door of ANY PetSmart without shaking.) So if you have a dog that was rescued from a violent home, that dog will remember. And it will generalize that memory.

Now, sometimes a dog will learn that its new male owner is fine. (Which is what happened with our rescue.) But have some other male come over? The dog'll be hiding under a table somewhere. Or under a bed.

5. Poor Training

Most (not all) rescues were not properly trained. Sometimes you'll get a rescue whose owner loved and adored it, but had to give the dog up because they were entering hospice or something horrible like that. But often a dog is a rescue because its first owner didn't raise it properly. So you have behavior issues like jumping on people, barking, or not being fully house-trained. And the older the dog and the longer they've been behaving "inappropriately" the harder it's going to be to train that dog to the proper behavior.

Add in the fear or aggression issues above, and it gets even more challenging.

6. You Don't Know What You're Getting

The final issue with rescue dogs is that many of them are mixed breed dogs. You think you're getting a Newfie mix and it turns out that you're getting a chow mix instead. (Not that there's anything wrong with chows, per se. We had four of them growing up and they were wonderful dogs because we raised them well.)

All those issues I talked about above in terms of temperament and energy level and intelligence and finding the right fit for you and the dog? Well, you often will have no idea what you're getting if you adopt a rescue. And you may be unpleasantly surprised by what you find.

🐾 🐾 🐾

Now, keep in mind that none of the above is the dog's fault. None of it. Dogs have no control over who chooses to raise them.

So don't make things worse by yelling at a rescue dog. (Or any dog for that matter.) You may have moments, when you get home and there's a big pile of you-know-what in the middle of the carpet, when you want to scream. Don't. The dog won't know why you're doing it, they'll just know that you screamed at them when you get home and they'll start to fear you and probably act up more.

Your training efforts will go much better if you can be calm and soothing and praise a dog for doing what you want it to do rather than yelling at it for doing what you don't want it to do. (Pavlovian conditioning and all that. Give the dog affirmation as it gets closer and closer to doing what you want it to do.)

(Of course, I say this as someone who has a breed that responds well to praise and treats. This gets back to knowing the breed you're taking on. If you have a dog that only responds to an alpha male—I'm not sure what breed that would be, but I'm sure there are a couple of them out there—then you better be that type of person or you are going to be in some serious trouble a year or so in.)

NAMING YOUR PUP

Think long and hard before you choose a name for your pup. I had to use my pup's name so many times during potty training that I got sick and tired of it.

Of course, with a name like Miss Priss, you can't really blame me, can you? You try saying, "Good job, Miss Priss. Way to do your business. That's a good girl, Miss Priss," about ten times a day and see how you feel about it. (Fortunately, she's smart enough to respond to the nice and generic Kiddo now.)

Realize that you will be using your pup's name for the next decade-plus. Every time you take your dog somewhere and someone asks, "Who is this?" you'll have to tell them. And, if you choose a ridiculous name like I did, you'll notice that slight pause before they say, "What a cute name!"

Mmhm. Why don't you say what you really think? "Dear God, did you really name your dog that?"

I read somewhere that you should give your dog a name that's either two words or two syllables. (At least I lucked into that part of it.) And also something fairly basic that can't be confused with other common words that you're likely to use around the dog. (So, don't name your dog Treat.)

Makes sense to me. All I know is you should choose a name you can say without wincing. (Although, sadly, I will say that the pup lives up to her name. Even covered in mud, she's a bit of a priss.)

Oh, and if you're going to go to the dog park, then maybe choose a name that you're okay being called, too. It's a weird fact that most people at the dog park will know the name of your dog, but not yours. Which means that often at the dog park, pup and I are greeted with "Miss Priss" or "Hi, Miss Priss." Well, she can't talk, so guess who answers to Miss Priss? Yep. Yours truly.

WHAT YOU'RE GOING TO NEED
FOR YOU

This is one of those chapters that was in the other book that is almost 100% applicable to anyone who has a dog anywhere.

You'll easily think of some of the stuff you need for your new pup. Dog bowl? Yep. Dog food? Yep. Toys? Yep.

But what about all the things you need for you? Such as:

1. Vacuum Cleaner

You may already have a vacuum cleaner, but do you have one that can handle the amount of hair that is going to come off that pup? Some breeds shed fur and some shed hair. I don't really know the difference. All I know is that sometimes I'll pet a dog at the dog park and my hand comes away covered in fine little hairs and I look down and my sweats are covered in that dog's hair, too. Whereas other dogs, like the pup, seem to shed in clumps instead.

Either way, you need something to clean that up with.

Also be sure to get a vacuum with an attachment that you can run along the baseboards and into the corners. You'll be amazed how much hair collects in those places.

2. Swiffer Sweeper

Or something similar that lets you pick up shed hair without having to use a vacuum. Turns out my pup is scared of the vacuum cleaner, as many dogs are, and it's much easier to use one of these than pull the vacuum out of the closet when I need to clean the bathroom or kitchen. I'd probably run it along the carpet, too, if my socks weren't so amazingly good at picking up the pup's hair.

3. Lint Brush

If you have a dog whose hair gets on your clothes, you might want to give yourself a quick swipe before you walk out the door. You may get used to the sight of every jacket you own being covered in fine little dog hairs, but your co-workers or that hot date you have may judge you harshly for walking around like a little chia pet.

🐾 🐾 🐾

There are a few other things you may need depending on how much time you spend outdoors with your pup and whether you take the pup to the park often.

4. Tissues and Hand Sanitizer

You may not need this one, but I certainly did. Puppies explore the world with their mouths. And sometimes that world is a disgusting, dirty place. If you want to teach your pup not to eat the disgusting things it finds, the best way to do so is to remove them from the pup's mouth. (Keep in mind, I have a gentle breed. If you have an aggressive breed, maybe don't do that.)

Well, after you remove a dead rodent from your dog's mouth, or a crawdad, or horse poop, or…well, you get the point, you will definitely want to wash your hands off. And you won't be able to run to the nearest restroom if you're out and about with your pup, so carry some wipes and hand sanitizer with you.

5. Lotion

A side effect of washing your hands as many times as I had to when I first had the pup is that your hands will get very dry and chapped. You're going to need lotion. (Of course, if your pup is anything like mine was, the pup will then try to lick the lotion off your hands, which sort of defeats the purpose, but you have to at least try.)

6. Sunscreen

I take the pup to the dog park almost every day. And we're there for close to an hour each time. I have to wear sunscreen. I love her, but I don't love the risk of skin cancer.

7. Better Outdoor Clothes

I learned very quickly after I got the pup that the outdoor clothes I had were not up to the task of walking around outside for an hour. My boots were cute, sure, and even waterproof, but they weren't meant to keep my toes warm while standing outside for half an hour in the middle of winter. My gloves weren't up to the task either.

Turns out the clothes I had were good enough for that quick walk to the car or that five minute wait for the subway, but they couldn't handle the prolonged exposure that came with taking the pup out in cold weather. (We went on an hour and half walk once in the middle of a snowstorm. And, yes, I am a very permissive puppy parent, but you should've seen how happy she was.)

🐾 🐾 🐾

This one MAY apply only to those in apartments, but it applies to me, too, since I spend far too much time in my pajamas.

8. Pajamas You Can Wear Outdoors

The thing about puppies is that when they need to go outside, they need to go out NOW. So when I lived in an apartment with the pup I had about two minutes to get dressed and out the door when pup woke me in the middle of the night with her plaintive little cry. That meant a complete overhaul in the pajamas department.

For example, in the winter, I started sleeping in thermal leggings so I could just throw a pair of sweats over them before I raced out the door. Otherwise I'd find myself outside in freezing temperatures with a pup that suddenly had a shy bladder and the wind cutting straight through my sweats to my skin.

This can even apply if you live in a house. I tend to hang out with the pup in the yard a lot. And I'm just visible enough to passing traffic and the neighbors that I have to wear something at least minimally presentable to strangers.

At least be prepared with a robe or something, because, house or apartment, you will find yourself outside in the middle of the night at some point whether to walk your pup or retrieve it.

WHAT YOU'RE GOING TO NEED
FOR THE PUP

You will need a lot of things for your puppy. I mean, a lot. There are seventeen items on this list and I probably missed a few.

1. A Collar Or Harness And A Leash

Even if you live in a house, you will occasionally take your dog somewhere with you. Most notably, the vet. If you live in an apartment, you will be walking that dog multiple times a day. And if you take the pup to the dog park you should at least have the dog on leash between your car and the park entrance. (And may find it convenient to put the dog on leash within the park if there's any sort of confrontation with another dog or you find that the pup doesn't want to get anywhere near the exit.)

Now, I know there are a few people reading this that think, "I don't need that. My dog'll be fine."

Well...you're wrong.

When I lived in an apartment, there was this family that brought home a cute little boxer pup. Adorable dog. But they never used a leash to walk that dog. And one day it made a beeline across the parking lot to say hi to my pup.

Fortunately, nothing happened. But it could've. The dog could've easily been hit by a car. (It was small and I doubt anyone would've seen it in time to stop.) Also, there was no guarantee that my dog was going to be friendly and with that dog off-leash it was all up to me to control the situation. (Which is not easy when you have a sixty-pound puppy straining at its leash to get to another dog and that dog is running circles around you.)

Whether you go with a collar or a harness will be up to you. I use a collar, but I know a lot of people prefer a harness. Pup generally doesn't pull much, so a collar works for us because there are less places for it to rub against her skin. But if she were one to pull a lot, I might choose a harness to spare her neck. Problem with that is that I've heard a harness makes it easier for the dog to pull you around.

You can also look into things like choke collars or gentle leaders, which help control a dog's pulling.

Best bet is to consult with your dog trainer to see what they recommend. (Although they are very likely to recommend the choke collar or gentle leader. My trainer recommended a gentle leader and I ignored him. The second trainer I spoke to recommended a choke collar. I also ignored him, although one advantage to a choke collar is a dog can't slip out of it.)

Also, know that your dog is going to grow. If you get a single-size collar, you need to keep checking it to make sure the pup hasn't outgrown it. There are horror stories of people who left a collar on a dog and the dog grew and the collar got embedded in the dog's skin. Don't let that happen.

Your dog's collar should always be loose enough for you to fit your fingers underneath.

If you're going to take your dog to dog parks or even day care (although mine takes off the collar when they get there), then also make sure the collar is one that can be removed easily. The kind that buckle like a belt are not going to work.

Why do you need to do that? Well…Turns out that sometimes when dogs are playing, the jaw of one dog will get caught under the collar of the other. If you don't remove the collar quickly, the dog who is caught runs the risk of breaking its jaw. (Hence the reason my day care removes all collars.)

Another thing to consider is what kind of leash you want to use. I prefer a fixed length, six-foot leash. It keeps the dog under control, but still allows a decent amount of room for them to sniff at things.

I find those long retractable leashes to be problematic. The owners never really seem to be in control of their dog and when dogs start playing and one is on a retractable leash the dogs get wound up easily, which is bad because the leashes on those things are too thin and can cause damage to the dogs or their owners. (And, yes, you will likely at some point get wrapped up in your or another dog's leash if you are out and about with your puppy.)

2. Food And Water Bowls

This is a pretty obvious one. You could just use a bowl you have laying around, I guess, but in general you'll want dedicated food and water bowls for your dog.

If you have a larger dog, consider getting an elevated holder for the food and water bowls. Larger dogs like mine can be prone to bloat and bending over to eat and drink from floor-level can make bloat more likely.

Also, and this is probably unique to Newfies, my pup used to love to spill her water bowl and lay in it. She doesn't do that if the bowl is in an elevated holder.

(Just be careful that you don't ever let any pieces of food get underneath it. I had this happen with the pup and she knocked the whole feeder over trying to get to one little piece of food. Made a complete mess and drenched the carpet.)

3. Blankets

You don't have to use blankets, but they certainly help keep the furniture more clean than if you don't use them. (At least that's if you lose the couch fight like I did.)

I also used to use blankets for her spot on the floor and in the car. It helped for her to know where her designated spaces were. When I'd take her to a park to meet my mom for lunch, I'd bring the blanket and she'd know where she was supposed to lay down.

She now has beds she sleeps on (that are covered in blankets), but I didn't actually get her a dog bed for probably the first three months until she was past her chewing on everything stage.

4. Dog Beds

You probably don't want to have one of these day one. (Did I mention yet that puppies explore the world with their mouths and will chew on almost anything?) But eventually it's a nice thing to have a bed for the pup to use. (I have four now. Yes, pup is spoiled as spoiled can be.)

I also cover each bed with an $8 throw blanket I buy from Big Lots to make it easier to keep her beds clean.

Know that your dog may not like every dog bed, so you're going to probably have to do a little experimenting before you find one that works. When pup was smaller I bought her a dog bed that was on sale that was all big and poofy. All she wanted to do was chew that thing to pieces.

I've found success with the Top Dog flat dog beds you can get at PetSmart. They're basically just big stuffed rectangles and pup is able to sleep with her head hanging over the side, which she seems way too fond of doing.

Your mileage may vary. The key is to experiment until you find something that works for you and your pup.

5. Food

An obvious requirement.

Puppies (actually, all dogs) can be very sensitive to changes in their diet. So your best bet is to start feeding the pup whatever it was eating before it came to you. Then you can slowly transition the pup to any new food by mixing old and new over the course of about a week. Increase the amount of the new food by a little bit every day until you've completely transitioned from the old food.

Also, this is somewhat obvious, but feed a puppy puppy food. The bigger the breed, the longer they're going to need to be on puppy food. For my pup they said 1-2 years of puppy food. (Helpful, I know. I started transitioning her at one year and kept her on a mix of puppy and adult food until she reached a year and a half.)

You can expect that the pup's food needs will change as it grows, too. There was a point where I was feeding the pup six cups of food a day! (Now she's down to about three.) Consult with your vet about what they recommend for your particular breed, age, and food type.

And keep an eye on your pup's figure. There are three spots you can check to make sure the pup isn't getting overweight: ribs, waist, and belly. You should be able to feel but not see the ribs. The waist should dip inward if you're looking from above. And the belly should curve upward towards the hips. (Google for images of what I'm talking about.)

Fat puppies are damned cute, but it's not good for them. Especially a bigger breed like a Newf. The more weight, the more stress on the joints. And for a dog that grows really fast that can be a very bad thing. Not to mention all the other health issues that come with being overweight.

And I'm assuming you'll be feeding bagged or canned dog food, but there are some folks who feed their dogs "real" food. If you're one of them, just make sure you're getting the pup everything it needs to thrive.

6. Treats

You'll very likely want treats to train your pup. For example, after the pup does its business outside, you may want to congratulate it and give it a treat. (I didn't do this every time with the pup because I didn't want her to think she could go outside, pretend to pee, and get a treat. I did give her one every time she pooped outside. Not that she ever pooped inside, thankfully.)

Even if you want to eventually use a clicker for training, you still need to build that association between the sound of the clicker and the notion of reward. (You do this by pairing the sound of the clicker with the treat until the pup has the two firmly associated. Good ol' Pavlov.)

I will admit, I over-treat the pup. She gets into the car without my assistance, I give her a treat. I go out to bring her in when she's barking and she comes inside without my having to grab her or leash her, I give her a treat. I need her to leave the dog park and she comes over to let me leash her up, I give her a treat.

As long as she isn't getting fat, I don't see the issue. She knows if she does what I need, she'll get a treat, and she likes treats enough to do what I need her to do. Win-win for us.

(We're talking small treats, by the way. The treats I use are training treats so probably the size of one knuckle on my finger, if that. For a dog her size, that's nothing.)

7. Toys

You will need toys. We'll go into more detail about this later, but puppies need things to chew and chase. You can either give them appropriate toys or watch them eat everything you love.

When I was training the pup, each time she picked up something she shouldn't chew on (like my books, my power cord, my chair), I'd take it away and give her one of her approved toys. She got the point eventually.

Toys are also a good way to bond with your pup. You throw the ball, the pup chases, it's fun.

8. Protective Gear

This will very much depend on the type of dog you have and what you're going to be doing with that dog.

The first winter when I had the pup, the temperatures were really, really cold. To the point that I worried about her paws freezing up while we were walking. I also wanted to protect her from all that de-icer the apartment building used, which can be hell on a dog's feet.

So I got her booties. Well…She didn't go for it. She would shake her foot and try to chew the booties off. We ended up just roughing it and I tended to walk through the snowy grass with her rather than keep her to the sidewalk when there was de-icer in play. (I know. I am a pushover.)

My friend has Chihuahuas. Those things can't go outside in the winter without their little sweaters on to protect them. Hell, I think they wear them inside, too, in the winter. They don't have the same thick coat that the pup does to protect them from the cold.

And it isn't just winter weather that matters, either. Certain breeds can get sunburnt in the summer. (Not the pup. That coat protects her delicate little skin. Which, by the way, is why you don't shave a dog like her in the hot months. Again, know your breed.)

And if you're going to take a dog out on a lake you may need floaties or a life vest. Pup loves to swim, but she does it from the shore of the lake so I've never hooked her up with anything like that, but I know a lot of folks who take their dogs out in their boat and do.

For the most part, dogs can get by just as they are, but at least give it some consideration if you're going to be in extreme temperatures or environments. (Sharp rocks when hiking, for example.)

9. Odor And Stain Remover

You WILL need this if you have a puppy. Pup was great about letting me know when she needed to go outside. (Sometimes this involved jumping on my lap and biting my hands like a crazy little dervish, but at least she was trying to let me know.) Even so, there were times I didn't get her outside in time and she ended up peeing on the carpet. (Puppy bladders are SMALL and when they need to go, they need to go NOW.)

In addition to those kinds of accidents, chances are your puppy will puke at some point in time. I was able to get pup to the point where if she did need to puke she'd puke into or onto whatever I held before her face, but that first time she needed to puke she ran around the entire apartment making heaving noises and avoiding me until she finally managed to jump up on the couch and puke right where I normally sit.

(And you thought parenting a new puppy was all puppy kisses and snuggle time? HA!)

So, whatever the cause, you are going to need odor and stain remover. And you need the kind that is designed to really, really remove that scent. Dogs have a helluva lot better sense of smell than us lowly humans and if you don't get the smell of pee out of your carpet, the dog will keep going back to that same spot over and over again.

Unsure if you've caught all the spots where your dog peed? (Especially an issue with smaller breeds.) Use a UV light.

10. Puppy Gate

If you want your dog to learn not to pee/poop in the house, the best bet is to start the dog in a smaller area first. Pup and I started with her in the kitchen and slowly worked our way out from there. She went from the kitchen to the kitchen and dining room. Then the kitchen/dining room/bathroom. Then she was finally allowed the living room. The reason you start with a smaller space is because the dog knows that the space belongs to it and therefore won't mess in its space.

Now, I will say, I don't think we ever did this with our dogs when I was growing up. Then again, we always had an older dog to show the younger dog what to do.

A puppy gate also comes in handy if you need to run somewhere and haven't crate-trained your dog. When pup was really little and she fell asleep, I'd gate her off in her space and then run to the store. Even if she woke up, there wasn't much she could do in the kitchen.

I recommend one of those puppy gates that is adjustable in size (mine could be as small as three feet wide and up to almost six feet wide) and that also can stand on its own rather than needing to be braced against two walls. That stand-alone ability was a life-saver for me. It made the gate much more versatile.

11. Crate

Now, if you're smart, you'll crate-train your dog. It's not a bad thing for a dog. For many dogs, their crate is their safe space.

They enjoy being in it. And, if you want to train them properly, that's how you want them to think about their crate. Don't shove them in there when they're being bad. Going to their crate should never be a punishment.

I didn't properly crate-train the pup. I was working from home and didn't need to and by the time I thought of doing so, she wasn't really into the whole idea. By then she was good enough being left to run free in the apartment that I didn't bother pushing the issue.

If you crate-train from day one, you will be much better off. And, especially if you plan on being gone for a whole workday, this may be the only way to leave your pup at home and have a home to return to at the end of the day.

Just because a dog likes its crate doesn't mean you should take advantage of that, though. Don't leave a dog in there for fifteen hours at a time. Even if the dog doesn't ultimately lose control and have to mess in there, it's just a cruel thing to do.

12. Benadryl

When I moved into a house with a yard it seemed like the pup immediately managed to find every wasp or bee there was. One day she came in with both of her ears swollen. The next day she had a big swollen lump under her right eye. The next day it was a lump on her nose.

The first time it happened, I ran her to the vet, worried that she was about to die from her throat swelling shut. He basically prescribed Benadryl and charged me $200 for the privilege. (Emergency vet.) The next time? I gave her two little Benadryl and watched the bite disappear over the next few hours.

Benadryl can also work to calm some dogs. When I drove the pup from Denver to DC, I'd give her a couple Benadryl in the morning before we started out. It helped mellow her out for six hours of cross-country driving.

(Of course, I consulted with my vet before doing so. You should too. And dosage is based on weight, so know what you're doing before you give a pup any medicine.)

13. Puppy Wipes

Not every dog loves a bath. Actually, most dogs probably do not love baths. Pup will happily swim in a puddle and loves a lake or stream, but get her anywhere near the bath tub and she acts like she's going to her execution. So, puppy wipes have come in very handy. I can notice that she's smelling a little funky (which happens often) and just wipe her down real quick. They're also great for dealing with minor dirtiness issues, like muddy paws.

14. Grooming Materials

Know your breed and know what kind of brushes, combs, etc. work for the type of coat your dog has. You should also know how often your dog needs to be brushed to keep its coat matt-free. With pup, I generally have to brush her at least a couple times a week, even more often if she decides to go running through the tall dry grass.

Common advice is to get your pup used to being groomed early. Sit them down for a few minutes each day and brush their coat and look at their ears and play with their paws.

I did this with the pup. And she will, if she's in a mellow enough mood, let me play with her paws, look at her ears, and even brush her. But if she's in a more active mode, she runs right out the door the minute a brush comes into view. My mom had a chow she did this with, too. That dog hated to be groomed for her entire life.

So, no guarantee that if you start them young they'll be okay with it. But, it is worth giving it a shot, because your dog will almost certainly need more grooming than you want to pay for at the local groomer's. (And, you may have something happen like I did where the pup develops a complete fear of being groomed at the groomer's and ALL of the grooming requirements fall on you.)

Also, one more reminder to know your breed. Pup is prone to getting matted right behind the ears. This was also true of the Great Pyrenees we had when I was growing up. That Pyrenees also had dew claws that required trimming on a regular basis or the claw would curl backward and embed itself into the paw. Not a good thing.

15. Ear Drops, Toothbrush/Toothpaste, Supplements
You probably don't want to start out with this stuff when you have a brand new puppy, but over time I've found myself buying all of the above for the pup. If you can manage to brush your dog's teeth on a regular basis, that is great. It will likely save you on vet bills down the road. I've tried, but pup spends so much time trying to lick the bacon toothpaste off the brush that I gave up.

I have ear drops for her, too. And I use them every once in a while. I'd use them more often, but every time I get the bottle out she runs for the hills and I have to track her down and wear her out before she lets me use them.

She does at least like her supplements. I have her on fish oil and glucosamine to help with her joints. We had a scare when she was about a year old where she pulled her back leg and the vet said supplements like that might help.

Read the labels before you use anything with your dog to make sure it's appropriate for a dog of that age and size. And consult with your vet before putting your dog on anything too weird.

16. No-Chew Spray
This stuff was a lifesaver for me. When pup was little she tried to chew everything. It's what puppies do. But I didn't need her chewing the drywall in my rented apartment. Nor did I need her chewing my wooden t.v. trays. Or the seatbelts in the car.

Well, a few sprays of bitter apple spray and she learned that was not what she was supposed to be chewing.

Better to train the dog not to chew something like that than to assume that you can just pull the dog away from chewing it whenever it starts chewing. You can't be there all the time, so you need to ingrain good habits in your dog.

And do keep in mind that some breeds actually like the taste of the spray. Newfies are one of those breeds. It smells a lot like rubbing alcohol, but pup would lick the stuff after I sprayed it! She did stop chewing, though, and that's what counted.

17. Towels

I assume you want your dog to do its business outside? Which means that wherever you live, house or apartment or ashram, that dog will be outside in all types of weather. And, if you aren't prepared, that dog will bring all the loveliness of outdoors back inside with them. Wet paws after rain. Snowy paws after snow. Muddy paws…

You aren't going to want to use your bathroom towels or kitchen towels to wipe your pup down, so dedicate a towel or two to the cause now and keep it somewhere within reach of the door.

PREPARING YOUR HOUSE

I didn't have kids when I got the pup, which means my house was not yet baby/puppy proofed. I assume that if you're reading this book, you're probably in the same boat. So look around and figure out what in your house is at puppy level. And then move it unless you want it chewed on at least once.

Pup is very good and I was there 95% of the time the first few months, but she definitely got into things. I had books on a bottom shelf of a bookcase and I think she got those books at least three or four times before I broke her of the habit of trying. I also had little knick-knacks on those lower shelves that I moved out of the way before she came.

Hide your shoes and socks, too. I used to just keep my shoes near the door, but pup loves shoes. (She tends to use them as a way to get my attention more than anything, instead of to chew on.) Now I keep all of my shoes in the closet or out of her reach.

Power cords are another one that pups seem to love.

Basically, anything on the ground or within reach of the pup's mouth is at risk. Move what you can.

ESTABLISH A ROUTINE

It's tempting when you get a new puppy to take some time off and spend it with the pup non-stop. Problem is, with puppies, just like with most things in life, you're better off starting off how you want to finish.

If you know you're going to have to crate the dog for work, then start at least crating the dog for a few hours a day and leaving home so the dog gets used to it.

When I first had the pup, I almost never left her alone. I'd run to the store while she was sleeping (which she then figured out and took to sleeping in front of the front door), but otherwise I was there all the time. Which meant that when it did come time for me to get away for a bit—say to meet a friend for lunch—she was not a happy pup.

I'd hear her crying through the door as I walked out to my car. Fortunately for me, she's a great dog and she never vented her frustration on my belongings, but that does happen. You leave behind an angry or frustrated dog and you come home to a shredded couch or garbage strewn throughout the house.

So, get your pup used to life as it's going to be as soon as you reasonably can.

This also applies to feeding times and sleep times. If you let the puppy set your schedule (so, say, you're up at five each morning letting the pup out), it's going to stay that way. Yeah, you may have to deal with some crying early on, but if you can do it, get the pup on your preferred schedule.

I'll note two things here. One, when the pup is brand new you just want to get the dog outside as soon as you hear it moving around, so this isn't possible right away. Two, if you live in an apartment, you may not be able to pull this off. Neighbors tend not to like crying puppies at three in the morning. (Can't imagine why...) And if you have a noisy neighbor who wakes up really early, like I did, the pup will wake up then, too. Say goodbye to sleeping in if that happens.

EXPOSE YOUR DOG TO DIFFERENT EXPERIENCES

One of the best pieces of advice I ever received was to get the pup used to traveling in the car. At the time I was given this advice, I didn't really see the need for it. I'd run the pup up to the park every few days or to PetSmart a couple times a week, but we were good walking around our apartment complex so we didn't need to drive anywhere every day.

Well, one job offer and a cross-country move later, I was so so so grateful that I'd driven the pup around in the car enough for her to travel well.

It isn't just traveling in the car either.

I knew a woman who had never left her dog alone in five years, but then suddenly had some health issues and needed to take the dog to day care and to boarding. Well, that did not work out well. The dog was an absolute wreck every time she took it in, because it had never been through that before.

When I had pup in training classes they also recommended exposing your dog to as many different types of people and dogs as you could in the first six months. I think the recommendation was fifty of each. (Easy to do in an apartment, let me tell you.)

This is so so true. Pup to this day gets too excited when she meets little kids because I kept her away from the brats in my apartment building. If she'd been around them more, she'd probably be much more chill with kids and my best friend could bring her daughter by the house.

I also saw this with pup and men in baseball caps. I guess we weren't around many men in baseball caps, because the first time she saw a guy at the dog park wearing a baseball cap she barked at him until I called her away.

So, variety. Let your pup see the wide range of people and dogs and places in this world and you'll have a much calmer and better behaved dog on your hands.

Another thing. Use it or lose it. It's great to expose your dog, but if you don't keep up with it, I think it probably loses its value. I know with us and walking on leash that the pup isn't as good now as she used to be. She's not terrible, but she pulls a lot more than she did when we were walking on leash every day four times a day.

THE GO BAG

I found this incredibly helpful when I lived in an apartment and had to be able to rush out the door without any notice. But I still use one when I take the pup anywhere. You may not need all of these items every time, but I think you'll find that it's nice to have them on hand when you do.

My go bag is a flat purse with multiple pockets that's small enough to be easy to wear all the time but big enough to fit everything I need.

What's in it?

1. Poop Bags

This is a must. If you're going to take your dog off of your property, be prepared to pick up after it if it decides to do its business. Sure, some places provide bags, but anyone who's been doing this for a bit can tell you two things. One, sometimes those dispensers run out of bags just when you need them. Two, you're never anywhere near one of those dispensers when your dog decides to go. You're better off always having a few poop bags with you and replenishing your supply next time you see a dispenser.

Also, always have a few extra bags. I actually carry a roll of a hundred in the very bottom of my bag that I almost never need. Why do you need to do this? 'Cause sometimes your pup gets sick and you end up needing four or five bags in one outing. Or you pup pukes and does its business in the same walk. Be prepared.

And, yes, it at all possible, you should pick up your dog's puke.

Why?

So someone else's dog doesn't eat it. You may not think it's a big deal, but wait until it happens to you and then your dog wants to give you a kiss five minutes later.

2. Treats
I already admitted that I tend to treat the pup to get the behaviors I want. When the pup was little she'd sometimes plop herself down and refuse to move. (It's called the Newfie Flop.) She would, however, move if I left a little trail of treats for her to follow. A helluva lot easier than trying to wrangle a resistant sixty-pound dog. (Although I also found that if I let her sit there for a minute or two and then started a countdown from twenty that she'd generally get up when I got to about three.)

I also use treats to bribe the pup to give a tennis ball back if she steals it from another dog. Or to look at me instead of a rabbit or squirrel. And to come to me when we're at the dog park and it's time to leave.

You don't have to use them, but it's nice to have another tool in the arsenal when you need it.

3. Tissues/Wet Wipes
You never know what your dog is going to get into out there in the big, bad world. Will your pup pick up something absolutely disgusting that you wrestle out of its jaws? Or what about the ball you just threw for your pup that was covered in saliva and dirt and who knows what else? Or what about wiping off your pup's face or paws when your pup gets muddy or slimed by another dog?

I'm very mellow about how dirty the pup and I get when out and about, but even I find myself reaching for tissues on a regular basis.

4. Keys

This is obvious, but you'll need your keys. (Believe it or not, when I first had the pup and lived in an apartment where the door didn't automatically lock, I forgot my keys on a regular basis because I was so in a rush to get the pup out the door. Which is better than when I came back to the apartment, unlocked the door, and left the keys in the door, which happened more than I'd like to admit. Puppy brain. It's real.)

5. Sunglasses/Hat

This is if you're going to be outside with your pup for any length of time. Once you're out there, it isn't a simple matter of just running back inside. So, if you need sun protection, make sure to take what you need with you when you walk out the door the first time.

6. Gloves

Same as with the sunglasses/hat. You may think you don't need gloves until you find yourself stuck outside with the pup for ten minutes instead of the two you were planning on. And, yes, this can happen even when you're running to the vet or the store with your pup.

7. Flashlight

This is really only for those that'll be outside at night with their dogs, which is generally the apartment-living folks. It's almost inevitable that if you walk a dog at night the dog will stop and do its business at a point as far away from the nearest light source as it can. Or will walk you through an area with no lighting where there's a pretty high possibility that other dogs have done their business and no one bothered to pick up.

ADDITIONAL ITEMS FOR
THE PARK

The go bag is something I take almost everywhere I go with the pup. But some locations require a few extra items.

I used to meet my mom for lunch at the local park when the pup was little. This isn't a dog park we're talking about, but an actual park. I also used to let the pup run around a group of soccer fields near my house when she was still too young to be around other dogs. (You need your pup to have all its shots before you really get out there and start mixing it up with other dogs because your pup is susceptible to getting really sick otherwise.)

So, what else would I take if I was going to spend more than a few minutes at the local park?

1. Water
I always liked to have a bowl of water there and available for the pup. Some parks have water and some don't, but most aren't equipped for you to let your pup drink.

There are tons of options out there for taking water with you. I have a great one for hiking that has a container and bowl in one and lets me drain the water back into the container when it's time to leave. I also used to have one that had two bowls and a container that all fit together as one unit and had a nice little carry handle.

Look around. Find what works for you.

I like to have one that's dedicated to the pup and that travels well. When we're not at a park, I have it in the back of the car for her to have water while we're on the road.

2. Toys

When my mom and I would go to the park, we'd be there for an hour or more. And you don't want a curious puppy at a park with nothing in her mouth. Why? Because she will find something to put in her mouth even if that means chewing on geese poop or glass. So bring toys. (And check the area you sit in for things like glass, cigarette butts, rocks, pine cones, etc.)

3. Blanket

I mentioned it before. Pup learned that the blanket was her space, so I'd bring one with me to the park and lay it out next to the picnic table so she knew where "her" spot was at the park. The other nice thing about using a blanket is that there's nothing on it that you didn't put there.

4. Phone

This should be a given, but when you have puppy brain anything can happen. Any time you take your dog with you beyond easy reach of your home, you should really have a phone. What happens if you break down on the side of the road? What you alone would do is probably not the same as what you will do when your pup's with you.

5. Wallet

Another easy one to forget with puppy brain. You may not think you need money, but you never know.

6. First Aid Kit

I have one in my car. For a long time I didn't. But you just never know what a puppy will get into and it's nice to be able to handle a minor medical issue on-site.

7. Tether

This was kind of a fail for us. For some reason, pup never realized she was on the tether and would run to the end of it and then jerk back. But if you have a dog that doesn't do that, this lets you have the dog in a prescribed area where it's free to run around. I think mine had a ten or twenty foot allowance, which is a pretty nice space for a dog.

ADDITIONAL ITEMS FOR
THE DOG PARK

I generally only take my go bag, phone, wallet, and keys when I go to the dog park, but some people like to bring their own toys and I've seen many people bring those ball-tossing sticks. They're a good idea if you're the least bit squeamish about touching muddy, spit-covered balls. (I'm not.)

Also, be very aware of what you're wearing. I tend towards hiking boots at my favorite dog park because it can be muddy for good portions of the year and not all of the trails the pup likes are paved. You should also wear appropriate clothing or sunscreen to protect your ears, nose, and fingers in the winter and ears and top of your head in the summer.

DOG PARK ETIQUETTE

I've now written an entire book about going to the dog park. (*Dog Park Basics*) If that's something you really want to do, then you're probably best off picking that book up. But I'll give you the ten second summary.

A dog park is a shared space and whether or not it's an enjoyable experience depends on everyone who goes there. So do your part. Pick up after your dog, control your dog, be friendly to others, respect others by keeping your dog from jumping and by asking before you give other dogs treats, and don't litter.

Also, be aware that there are safety issues with going to a dog park. In addition to paying attention to dog behavior and avoiding conflict between two dogs, keep your dog on leash until it's in the park and consider leaving young children at home. Dogs can and do get over-exuberant when they're playing and it's fairly common for them to run into humans while playing.

Above all, remember that the dog park is for the *dogs* to play, so try to create the best place for them to do so that you can.

EXERCISING YOUR DOG

If you live in a house with a yard, this is much easier than if you live in an apartment. If you have a small breed dog, this is also easier than if you have a large breed. And, of course, some dogs are just much more high energy than others.

When a pup is young, it's growing. You need to pay attention to how much exercise is good for it versus how much can be damaging. I was told that my pup shouldn't really exercise more than she would get in a yard at home until she was two. This is because her breed grows fast enough that over-exercising her could cause stress on her joints which could lead to health issues. (I also learned that she should avoid stairs as much as possible for the first six months to help keep her from developing hip dysplasia.)

Because of that, I didn't go hiking with the pup until she turned two. (And once I read that article about the stairs I stopped letting her climb up the stairs in my apartment building.)

At the same time, puppies need exercise. And if you live in an apartment, walking your dog outside to do its business probably isn't going to be enough. Pups need to be able to run on occasion.

That's where dog parks come in handy. Or long walks. Or both.

If you live in a house, taking your dog for a walk at a nearby park or around the neighborhood can be good, too. It helps teach the dog to walk on leash. (Something that's very easy to overlook if you live in a house and don't go places often.) And it gives an opportunity for you to bond with the dog.

Keep in mind that a dog that is properly exercised and adequately entertained is also going to be less destructive. So, win-win. Get out there and spend some quality time with your pup while letting it stretch its legs a bit.

How will you know when your dog needs some exercise? Well, in my case, the pup would start running crazy circles around the apartment when she'd been cooped up inside for too long. Pretty clear indicator that she needed to get outside and run for a bit.

TOYS – GENERAL

I mentioned it before. Toys are essential for raising a well-behaved pup. Puppies explore the world with their mouths and if you don't have something appropriate to give the pup to chew on, it will find something inappropriate to chew on.

I give the pup toys with a variety of textures. Her toys range from Nylabones that are very hard to soft stuffed toys. I also have rubbery toys for her. And I also try to find toys with different sounds and textures, too. She has toys that squeak, toys that crinkle, toys that grunt, etc. She'll develop favorites here or there, but eventually she works her way through all of them.

Keep in mind, you MUST monitor your pup when it's playing with toys. A puppy can be great with a toy for days or weeks and then you find the thing torn to shreds and you're wondering where the squeaker that was inside the toy is now and whether you should call the vet or not.

Pup had a hedgehog she absolutely loved. She'd sort of gum the thing, but mostly she just slept on it. Fine. Great. Then one day I noticed that her poop was full of black string. I grabbed the hedgehog, and, sure enough, pup had started pulling out the toy's fur, one string at a time. That was the beginning of a phase where she tried to pull the hair out of every single toy she owned. I even had to behead one of her toys because of it. (Better that than having her swallow more hairs.)

Another type of toy she wasn't good with was rope toys. She'd pull the strings out of those, too. She could play with them if I was there with her and able to stop her when she started pulling, but I could never leave her alone with them.

She's better about it now and I do leave her alone with toys, but she can still surprise me. One day I left for an hour longer than normal and came home and she'd pulled the stuffing out of one of her favorite toys. So you just never quite know.

And with a puppy? I can almost guarantee that eventually that toy will get destroyed in one way or another. (Hint: It helps if you get comfortable using a needle and thread to patch up minor, and not so minor, rips. Pup tended to chew away at the eyes on her toys so she ended up with a lot of toys with missing faces after I sewed them back up.)

TOYS—THE NOISE ISSUE

This mostly applies to those who live in apartments, but it could also apply if you have roommates who aren't as enamored with your pup as you are or young children/babies around the house who might not sleep as heavily as you'd like.

See, problem with most dog toys is that they come with squeakers in them. Which means that if your dog is playing with its toy, it's making lots and lots of noise, too. Fine in the middle of the day. Not so fun if it's two in the morning.

When I first had the pup, I'd have her sleep in the bedroom with me. And, to calm her down, I'd bring a few of her toys in there with us. Which worked for the most part. Except she sometimes liked to wake up in the middle of the night and start playing with one of her toys. I quickly learned that I had to be choosy about which toys I allowed in the bedroom.

It didn't mean an automatic ban on every toy that had a squeaker. She never did figure out that some of her stuffed toys could also squeak. It did mean banning all her rubbery toys. Have you ever heard puppy teeth scraping against rubber at two in the morning? Almost as bad as fingers on a chalkboard.

So pay attention to how noisy your pup's toys are and think about hiding the ones that will wake up the neighbors or kids until morning.

TRAINING YOUR PUP

When I was growing up, we didn't really take our dogs anywhere, so we never had them formally trained. We did train one dog eventually because she must've started being a problem somehow. But we never trained any of the others and it was probably too late by the time we got around to it with the dog we did train. Now, looking back on it, I think all of our dogs could've probably benefited from a basic puppy class.

If you live in an apartment or plan to take your dog out and about a lot, you should definitely make sure your dog is trained to follow basic commands. First of all, make sure the dog walks well on a leash. That means not pulling like a maniac and choking itself everywhere you go. Second, make sure your dog will listen to you in a busy or chaotic setting.

I am NOT an advocate of some of the training philosophies out there. Pup recently developed a fear of going into buildings so I thought I'd call in a trainer to help us work on that. He wanted to start with training her to walk on leash. (Even though she already does just fine at that.) His theory on walking your dog on leash was that your dog should constantly be looking to you for a cue as to what it should be doing and should immediately respond to your slightest twitch.

Now, that's fine for police dogs, which is what he used to train, but for my pup? No. When I take her somewhere it's as much for her enjoyment as for mine. And pup does obey me, but she also looks around and occasionally stops to sniff something or other. That's okay, because when I need her to move on, she does.

So be sure to find someone who shares your puppy parenting philosophy if you do decide to train your pup.

And, again, know your breed. I read very early on that Newfies are very intelligent and occasionally very stubborn dogs that are eager to please and respond to praise. The book I read said that the sooner you train a Newfie the better off you are, so I had her in puppy training classes at four months old. And boy am I glad I did.

So, what commands did I find really useful?

1. Look At Me
This is a very simple command that basically directs the dog's attention to your face. I found this command incredibly useful when I was walking the pup and I saw something I knew she'd react to, like, for example, a rabbit. I'd say, "Look at me" and she'd immediately turn and stare at my face and I could direct her away from the distraction. I just used it the other day, too, when she was barking at some dog she wanted to play with. I pulled out a treat, held it by my nose, and she immediately turned and watched me instead of barking at that dog.

It does work better if you distract your dog before it sees whatever you don't want it to see.

2. Sit
This is one of the more obvious ones that I think everyone knows. If you're in a store or at a restaurant or at a hotel, it's nice to be able to tell your pup to sit and have them wait patiently for you to take care of whatever it is you need to do.

3. Leave It
This command saved me when the pup was in her "I'll bite you to let you know I need to go out" phase. I was at my wit's end

with that. (If you don't know already, puppy teeth are sharp as hell and hurt very, very much.)

This command is usually taught as a way to get a dog to ignore something they want to eat or chew on. But once a dog learns leave it, it can basically be used to tell them to stop a behavior, too. I even use it to get the pup to stop barking.

Also, good to use in conjunction with the drop it command.

4. Drop It

If you aren't fast enough to tell your pup to leave it, you'll need to use drop it to get the pup to drop whatever is in its mouth. If your pup has a sense of humor like mine does, it'll drop it, wait two seconds, and pick it back up, so I always pair "drop it" with "leave it."

5. Stay

A handy one if you need the pup to stay in one spot while you go do something else. Works best if the pup can still see you when you move away from it. (If I tell the pup to stay and then leave the room, which I do often when she's in the office and I just need to go grab something, she eventually gets curious and comes to find me.)

6. Come

If you're going to take your dog out into the world, you need this command. If you're walking a dog on leash, you may not use it often, so it may not be very effective when you do need it. (That would be when the pup slips its collar and dashes off towards a busy street.) But at least train the dog on it.

And pay attention when your trainer tells you to use a "high value treat." I stopped doing this and basically had to re-train the pup on the command. I now have little salmon bits that I pretty much only use when it's time for the pup to leave the dog park and I need her to come back to me to get leashed up.

Also, don't feel like you have to do things the way everyone else does. For example, I have a specific whistle I use for the pup when we're at the dog park, so I almost never actually use the word "come" to call her back to me. You'll find that if you work with your dog, you'll start to form your own little sets of commands and behaviors that work for the two of you.

(I also use a "hold" command for her when I need her to wait to get out of the car. It's accompanied by my physically blocking her from leaving the car, but when I say hold and put my hand out, she doesn't try to get around me.)

🐾 🐾 🐾

There are other commands out there. *Heel* can be a nice one to use. I'm lucky because pup will naturally walk next to me if I pull her leash closer, so I don't technically make her heel. Especially since it doesn't matter to me which side she walks on as long as she walks well.

Go to your bed is another nice one that people use to get their dog out of the way when needed. And, of course, there are all the tricks you can train your dog to do.

I never saw the need to make my dog learn tricks, so I never taught her to shake or roll over or any of those. Problem with that is that we run into strangers and they expect her to be able to shake hands before they give her a treat. So they offer her a treat and say, "shake," and she just keeps sitting there staring at them, patiently waiting for them to give her the treat while they keep trying to get her to shake.

So, you know, maybe teach your dog to shake so other people will give it treats more easily.

PULLING CRAP OUT OF
YOUR PUP'S MOUTH

Even with the best-trained pup (okay, so maybe not with the BEST-trained pup), you are going to eventually have to pull something disgusting out of your pup's mouth. I mean, sure, you *could* let the dog eat whatever it is. Problem is, that may mean an emergency visit to the vet or it'll mean that your dog gets a taste for whatever it is and keeps eating the damned things. Not good.

When pup was little and she'd get ahold of something she shouldn't, I would pull it out of her mouth. Remember those toys I said might get destroyed? Well, one night pup was coughing a little. I reached into her mouth and pulled out a big hunk of stuffing that was in the back of her throat. The next day, I pulled a six-inch string out of her mouth and throat.

Those were things in the house. It doesn't include the rocks, pinecones, rabbit poop, leaves, dead animals, horse poop, geese poop (notice a theme there), grass, sticks, and who-knows-what-else that we found outside.

Now, if you live in an apartment, you will likely see your pup pick up all of these things while you're out walking. If you live in a house? Maybe supervise the pup while it's in the yard until you're sure it's smart enough not to eat rocks. (And, yes, when pup was first with my mom, she did try eating the rocks.)

If you don't want to touch whatever it is, you can generally pry the dog's jaws apart and direct their mouth toward the ground and let whatever it is drop out.

And, of course, know what breed you're dealing with. Pup didn't like my taking things out of her mouth, but she let me. Other breeds? You might not want to try that with them. And if you do do so, you need to start with the dog when it's a pup. Don't try that with an adult dog that isn't used to it.

PUKE AND POOP

While we're on the topic of disgusting things, chances are your dog is going to puke at some point. And it will definitely poop. If you're really unlucky, the dog will also get diarrhea indoors.

(I am insanely lucky in this respect. For a while there pup and I were in a fifth floor apartment. She woke me one night, waited for me to get dressed, waited for us to take the elevator, waited for us to get out of the building and around the corner, and then had diarrhea. Most dogs are not like that. You'll only know your pup has a sick stomach after it's been sick.)

So, puking. When pup was little she would sometimes eat too fast. And what happens when a pup eats too fast? Well, about a minute or two later, the pup pukes up a nice little pile of wet, gross dog food. And then, pups being pups, tries to eat it again.

(Solution: Feed the pup in smaller amounts or use something to slow their eating. Also, if you wet the food in advance or heat it a bit that makes it a little more digestible.)

Also, if you let your dog eat things it shouldn't, it may just puke them back up. I had a night with the pup where she woke in the middle of the night gagging. Turns out she'd eaten a whole stick at day care and proceeded to puke it back up in about fifty little pieces. (For some reason, my family didn't appreciate me texting them a photo of it...Can't imagine why.)

So, your dog will likely puke at some point. Clean it up, figure out what caused it, and move on.

Your dog will also likely have loose stools at some point. You can do things to make this less likely to happen. For example, some dogs get sick to their stomach when they're stressed. Solution? Try not to stress out your dog or give it something like Benadryl if you know it's going to be in a stressful situation.

As I mentioned before, changing up your pup's food will also sometimes lead to loose stools. As much as you can, keep what you feed your pup consistent. This includes treats. And, if you do have to change the pup's food, do it over the course of about a week instead of abruptly switching the pup to a new brand of food.

And then there's stomach illness. Pup had giardia twice in the first six months. And she had some other infection a few months after that that the vet described as like having little microscopic fishhooks digging into your skin.

If it's an infection like that, the only solution is to get your dog into the vet and on medication. But if it's just stress or something bad they ate, you can try boiled chicken and rice for a day or so and see if that clears it up. I get that Jasmine Rice at the store, throw a frozen chicken tender in with about a cup of the rice, and cook according to the bag instructions. And then I feed it to the pup for about a day until it's all gone. Usually clears up whatever it is. If not, we go to the vet.

A GOOD VETERINARIAN IS
WORTH THEIR WEIGHT IN GOLD

I love my vet. I was insanely fortunate to have him as my vet when I first had the pup, because we were there probably once a week.

When I brought the pup home she had a sinus infection. (It is not normal for a dog to have green snot coming out of their nose.)

Then she got an eye infection. (I had to give her drops twice a day. Not easy when she figured out my tricks after just one attempt.)

Then she got giardia.

Then she kept licking the hell out of her butt and we figured out her anal glands needed emptying. (Now that I let her eat grass all the time that is thankfully no longer an issue, but for a while there we had to go in every three months or so to get them emptied.)

Then I thought she'd broken her tooth. (She hadn't. It just turns out that when your pup loses the back puppy teeth they look very, very different from when your pup loses its front puppy teeth.)

Then she got giardia again.

Then she was sick to her stomach, but for no apparent reason.

Then she was supposed to get spayed, but failed the blood test.

Then she got spayed.

Then she got a horrible urinary tract infection. (I blame it on the groomer cutting the hair down there back so far that she had nothing to protect her.)

And that was all in the first three months I owned her.

(Anyone who thinks that puppies are cheap or easy is either lucky as hell or deluded.)

The great thing is that for almost all of those visits I had a vet that charged a reasonable price, was able to see us same-day, and was great with the pup. He'd get down on the floor and play with her before he'd start the exam so that she loved coming to see him.

When we moved, I obviously had to switch vets and, man, oh man…

Let's talk $600 for a vet visit to diagnose a urinary tract infection that was visible to the naked eye. And then giving the pup a test she'd already had because it was free under the damned plan I signed up for that brought the cost of that visit down to a mere $400.

Oh, and at a place with small rooms where they took an hour to see you and then, when they did come in, started the visit off with a rectal temperature without so much as a "how do you do." Poor pup. She hated that place. It's a wonder she let me take her there after that first visit.

So, find a good vet. As your dog gets older, hopefully you'll be at the vet less and less. But if you do have to go in, you want it to be as pleasant an experience as possible.

SPAY OR NEUTER YOUR DOG

Unless you plan to breed your dog (and actually know what the hell you're doing), get your dog spayed or neutered. If you have a female dog and don't spay her, you'll be dealing with her going into heat. One, it's gross. The dog bleeds all over your house while it's happening. (Or you have to put the dog in diapers until it's over.) Two, your dog may get pregnant whether you want it to or not.

We had a dog that wasn't spayed. She got out when she was in heat and found her way down a few houses to some willing male dog and, next thing you knew, we had a little puppy to raise. (Only one, thankfully.)

It seems like a cool idea to have your dog have puppies, but it's not.

Also, your dog will be more prone to certain illnesses if you don't spay it.

With male dogs, the issue is one of aggression. An unneutered male dog is going to be more aggressive than one that's neutered.

And, if you think you want to take your dogs to day care or board them, many places won't allow an unspayed/unneutered dog in day care.

RIDING IN THE CAR

Even if you don't take your dog on trips or to the park or to the pet store, you will still have to take your dog to the vet at some point. (You damn well better...)

It's a good idea to get your dog used to traveling in the car. You never know when it'll be needed. Of course, my pup is in the car daily because we go to the dog park daily. And she's driven cross-country with me, too. So the below tips are more geared towards that level of riding in the car, but take what works for you.

I will say, of the list below, keeping the windows up most of the way and making the dog ride in the back are pretty much musts in my book.

So, what should you consider?

1. Create A Space For Your Dog To Sit Without Interfering With Your Driving

The first day we brought the pup home from the pet store she weighed seventeen pounds and spent the entire ride standing on my lap as I drove the car. That clearly wasn't going to last. (She's now ninety-five pounds.)

So, about three weeks after I got her, I started making her ride in the back of the car. Did she want to? No. But she adjusted. And she's spoiled, so she literally has the whole back of the car to herself. I took out the back seats and replaced them with a little dog bed for her.

The key, though, is that she can't get into the front of the car and interfere with me when I'm driving. And that's what you really need to consider. Because it's not safe for you or the dog if you get distracted while driving.

Some people put crates in the back of their cars or use doggie seatbelts or dog screens. Do what works for you and will keep your pup safe while you're driving.

2. Don't Let Your Dog Hang Its Head Out the Window
I know, everyone does it, so why can't you? Problem is, a dog can hurt either its eyes or nose by doing this. Think about it. The dog has its face hanging out there and you're driving fifty miles an hour. Well, stuff is hitting your pup's face at at least fifty miles an hour if not more. Ouch.

Also, be sure to engage the kid lock feature on your windows when driving around with your dog. My mom had a situation where one of her dogs put his head out the window and then put his paw on the window button and rolled the window up on his neck to the point where it was choking him. It was a nightmare moment for her and for him.

I've forgotten to engage the kid lock once or twice myself and found myself driving onto the highway while pup's rolling the window all the way down in the back seat. I do not need her jumping out of a car going seventy, but you try moving a dog away from a window while trying to merge into highway traffic and also roll the window back up at the same time.

Not fun.

3. Make Water Available
Even though the pup and I generally drive to the dog park or my grandma's these days, I still make sure there's water available for her in the car. After much trial and error and damp floor mats, I've finally settled on using a no-spill bowl for her. (She hates it, but it does what it's supposed to, which is let her drink water if she needs it while keeping my car dry.)

If you're traveling for long periods of time, water is essential.

4. Consider Adding Padding Or A Bed

Because I took out the back seats in my car, there are gaps and screws and other unpleasant things now exposed on the floor of my car. Things that could hurt the pup if I hadn't covered them over with blankets and dog beds.

Also, on a longer drive, your pup will likely want to lie down. Give the pup a comfortable place to do that in.

5. Provide Toys On Long Trips

When pup and I drove to DC, I didn't give her toys to play with the first day. Well...she entertained herself by chewing on the seatbelt. (Pups use their mouths for everything.)

When we used to commute half an hour to her day care she'd start crying when we were stuck in rush hour traffic. Toys or Nylabones or whatever were essential to distract her.

6. Set A Comfortable Temperature

Dogs have a different way of keeping cool than humans do, and I think it's better to set the temperature to fit your pup's needs than to set it to fit yours. Which means the car is generally a bit cooler than I would prefer. But pup can't add and take off layers the way I can.

7. Don't Leave Your Dog Alone In the Car

You hear the news stories every year about someone who leaves a baby in a car and the kid dies. Your car can quickly become an oven when closed up. Just think about what it's like when you park your car outside in summer and leave it there for an hour. Well, put a dog in a situation like that and you'll kill it. So don't.

Now, having said that...

Pup and I had to drive alone cross-country and we had to do enough driving each day that I needed to stop to use the restroom while driving. So, I've had to leave her in the car for a minute or two before. If you do have to, do it for as little a period of time as possible, preferably no more than about five minutes. Roll the windows down enough to get the pup air but not enough to let the pup jump out. And park in as much shade as you can find.

Cold weather isn't quite as high risk as hot weather, but if it's cold enough and you leave the pup in the car long enough, the pup can die that way, too. So, best bet is to not leave your dog alone in a car for any length of time regardless of the weather.

FEEDING YOUR DOG HUMAN FOOD

You can do this and I've definitely done it over the years, but I'd recommend trying not to for as long as possible.

I managed to not feed the pup human food for the first two years. (Except for rice and chicken when she was sick and carrots when she was teething.) Nice side effect of that was that she didn't even notice my food. I could leave a plate of bacon sitting on a tray in the front room and she wouldn't even bat an eye at it. It also meant no begging and, with a Newf, no drooling.

I have since gotten away from the very good start I had and do feed her bits of my food now, but she'll still only take food I give her and leave my food alone otherwise.

If you do feed your dog human food, pay attention to those lists of what you shouldn't feed your dog. Dogs have sensitivities to foods that humans don't. For example, dogs can't have chocolate. Or grapes or raisins. (You'd think no one would try to feed a dog a grape, just because, a grape, really? But I had to recently stop someone from feeding the pup a grape. And celery. When there were carrots sitting right there…)

Onions and garlic are also things you shouldn't feed your dog. As are sugar-free foods that include xylitol. And no beer or other alcohol.

You'd think that you won't feed your dog any of the above, but I've had to stop myself a few times. I'll fry up potatoes and use garlic salt and then realize that pup shouldn't have the garlic. Or go to give her some stew and realize that it used onions and garlic.

Now, the quantities required to really do damage are pretty high, but your best bet is to avoid these types of foods altogether. There are others, too. This wasn't a comprehensive list. So if you're going to feed your dog human food, look it up and know what to avoid.

WHAT TO DO FOR
A SICK STOMACH

I mentioned chicken and rice before, but there are other things you can give a dog that has a sick stomach.

1. Tylan Powder

I don't think this is very common, but my vet prescribed it for the pup at one point when she had generally loose bowels and we couldn't find a specific cause. It worked amazingly well. And I kept using it when we were in DC and she was exposed to the water there. She'd start to get a little off, I'd give her a bit, and boom, she was fine again. I saw when I was looking it up that for some breeds that are really prone to digestive issues, this is what the owners swear by. Some of those dogs were on this for their entire lives.

2. Pumpkin

This was another one I used often when the pup was little. It works for any stomach issues—constipation or diarrhea. I had the pup on two tablespoons a day for a while and it really did help.

3. Chicken And Sticky Rice

I didn't mention this part above, but you want to slightly overcook the rice to the point where it's a little gummy. Just boil up the chicken with the rice.

This also worked well recently for a friend who had a new rescue pup that refused to eat.

MAKE FRIENDS

This was far more important when I lived in an apartment than it is now with a house, but it really will help you if you make friends with the people around you.

In an apartment, it's essential to make friends with the management of your building. Pup was a real trooper, but she still had her moments of barking at someone on the elevator or barking when she got scared by someone. Well, management knew us and knew this wasn't how she normally was, so they let it slide when she acted up.

If they hadn't known us? We might've been kicked out of our building.

Same goes with neighbors. If they know and like your dog and one day it gets out of control with barking, they'll forgive you. If they don't know you, they may call management or animal control.

Helps, too, if it turns out you have the type of dog that runs away from home. A neighbor who knows you and your dog will help bring the dog back or at least let you know. If they don't know you or like you, they probably won't do a thing to help.

Make allies before you need them.

DEALING WITH CHILDREN

I don't have kids. Which means that the only kids pup is exposed to are strange kids that we run into out in public. This used to happen all the time when I lived in an apartment and she was little.

Problem with most kids is that they don't know how to interact with dogs. They will try to get the pup to jump up by bringing a hand down at the pup's face. Or scream and run away when they see a dog—playing, they think, but in a way that upsets the dog.

I also had one little girl in our building who was a terror. She rode a scooter right up to the pup's face, scaring her so bad, pup peed herself. She also decided to rename the pup, and got down on all fours and barked at her. Oh, and she also did that thing with holding her hand right above the pup's face and jerking it away fast.

That girl was a nightmare. But if pup had ever bit her? No one would've cared that the girl had taunted and harassed her. They would've all blamed the pup for reacting.

I had another kid who would silently follow us around and then start petting the pup without speaking or letting her know he was there.

So even if you don't have kids at home, you're going to be faced with kids trying to play with your dog and failing miserably. That doesn't even cover the kids who will harass your dog when it's in your yard.

You can try to keep your pup away from kids, but then you end up with a dog that doesn't know how to act with kids and gets all excited when they're around. (Mine starts barking and trying to play with them. Not a good thing when she's twice their size.)

If you do have kids at home, you need to train those kids how to behave with a dog. Pulling on ears or tails is not okay. Screaming in a dog's face is not okay. Taking food or toys from a dog may not be okay depending on the dog.

And, yes, you need to train the dog, too. But don't overlook the kids angle.

CONCLUSION

So that's about it.

It seems a bit daunting when you read all of it, but taking pup on was probably the best thing I've done so far in my adult life.

Remember, with a puppy you're going to get out of it what you put into it. If you love and care for your pup and spend quality time with it, you will have a creature that is loyal and loving in a way that few others are capable of. If you ignore your pup and don't care for it or, worse, abuse it, you'll have a distrustful, potentially dangerous animal on your hands. It's up to you how your pup turns out.

(Much like parenting. Certain breeds are predisposed to be a certain way, but how you treat your pup is going have a huge impact on how your pup turns out.)

Keep your patience. Don't cry. Don't give up.

Praise good behavior. Ignore the bad.

And enjoy. Time will go by far too fast and before you know it you're looking at your quiet, older dog wondering where your puppy went.

ABOUT THE AUTHOR

Cassie Leigh is the proud puppy parent of an adorable and incorrigible Newfoundland named Miss Priss.

She has lots of opinions and a few useful suggestions about surviving those first months of parenting a puppy. It's not necessarily easy, but it is definitely worth it.

Made in the USA
Lexington, KY
09 January 2017